Experiment!

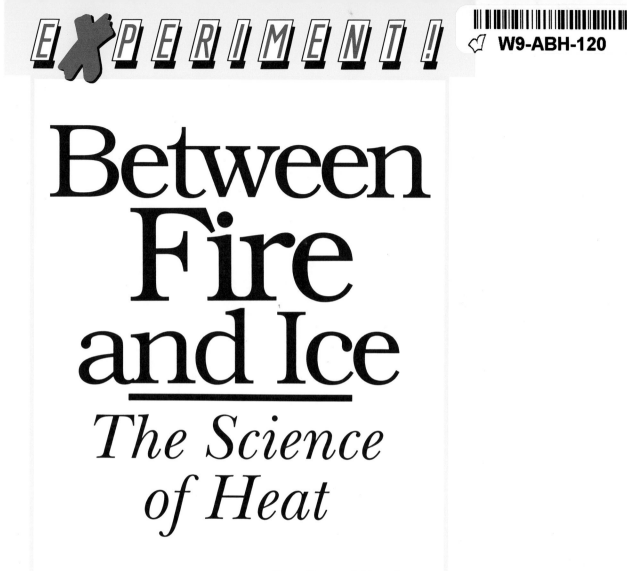

Between Fire and Ice

The Science of Heat

Dr. David Darling

DILLON PRESS
New York

Maxwell Macmillan Canada
Toronto

Maxwell Macmillan International
New York   Oxford   Singapore   Sydney

Photographic Acknowledgments

All photographs have been reproduced courtesy of Unicorn Stock Photos.
Back cover: Marie Mills/David Cummings (top); David P. Dill (bottom)
Jeanne Boden, 8; Betts Anderson, 12; Marie Mills/David Cummings, 17; Tom McCarthy, 18, 32; Martha McBride, 19, 42; A. Gurmankin, 22; Herbert L. Stormont, 24; Daniel J. Olson, 27; Jay Foreman, 35; Greg Greer, 37; Aneal Vohra, 39; Martin R. Jones, 42; David P. Dill, 46

Library of Congress Cataloging-in-Publication Data
Darling, David J.
    Between fire and ice : the science of heat / by David Darling.
        p. cm. — (Experiment!)
    Includes index.
    Summary: A collection of experiments exploring heat and its effects.
    ISBN 0-87518-501-0
    1. Heat—Juvenile literature. [1. Heat—Experiments. 2. Experiments.] I. Title. II. Series: Darling, David J. Experiment!
QC256.D37   1992
536—dc20   91-40966

Copyright © 1992 by Dillon Press, Macmillan Publishing Company

Dillon Press
Macmillan Publishing Company
866 Third Avenue
New York, NY 10022

Maxwell Macmillan Canada, Inc.
1200 Eglinton Avenue East
Suite 200
Don Mills, Ontario M3C 3N1

Macmillan Publishing Company is part of the Maxwell Communication Group of Companies.

First edition
Printed in the United States of America
10 9 8 7 6 5 4 3 2 1

Contents

What is Science?

Imagine gazing to the edge of the universe with the help of a giant telescope, or designing a future car using a computer that can do over a billion calculations a second. Think what it would be like to investigate the strange calls of the humpback whale, dig up the bones of a new type of dinosaur, or drill a hole ten miles into the earth.

As you read this, men and women around the world are doing exactly these things. Others are trying to find out how the human brain works, how to build better rocket engines, and how to develop new energy sources for the twenty-first century. There are researchers working at the South Pole, in the Amazon jungle, under the sea, in space, and in laboratories on every continent. All these people are scientists. But what does that mean? Just what is science?

Observation

Science is simply a way of looking at the world with an open, inquiring mind. It usually starts with an observation. For example, you might observe that the leaves of some trees turn brown, yellow, or red in fall. That may seem obvious. But

to a scientist, it raises all sorts of interesting questions. What substances in a leaf cause the various colors? What happens when the color changes? Does the leaf swap its green-colored chemical for a brown one? Or are the chemicals that cause the fall colors there all the time but remain hidden from view when the green substance is present?

Hypothesis

At this stage, you might come up with your own explanation for what is going on inside the leaf. This early explanation—a sort of intelligent guess—is called a working hypothesis. To be useful, a hypothesis should lead to predictions that can be tested. For instance, your hypothesis might be that leaves always contain brown, yellow, or red chemicals. It is just that when the green substance is there it masks or covers over the other colors. This is a good scientific hypothesis because a test can be done that could prove it wrong.

Experiment

As a next step, you might devise an experiment to look more deeply into the problem. A well-designed experiment allows you to isolate the factors you think are important, while controlling or leaving out the rest.

Somehow you have to extract the colored chemicals from a batch of green

leaves and those from a batch of brown leaves. You might do this, for example, by crushing the leaves and putting a drop of "leaf juice" partway up a narrow strip of blotting paper. Hanging the blotting paper so that it dips in a bowl of water would then cause different colored chemicals from the leaf to be carried to different heights up the paper. By comparing the blotting paper records from the green leaves and the brown leaves, you would be able to tell which chemicals were the same and which were different. Then, depending on the results, you could conclude either that your first hypothesis seemed right or that it needed to be replaced.

Real Science
What we have just described is perhaps the "standard" or "ideal" way to do science. But just as real houses are never spotlessly clean, real science is never quite as neat and tidy as we might wish. Experiments and investigations do not always go the

way scientists expect. Being human, scientists cannot control all the parts of an experiment. Sometimes they are surprised by the results, and often important discoveries are made completely by chance.

Breakthroughs in science do not even have to begin with an observation of the outside world. Albert Einstein, for instance, used "thought experiments" as the starting point for his greatest pieces of work—the special and general theories of relativity. One of his earliest thought experiments was to imagine what it would be like to ride on a light beam. The fact is, scientists use all sorts of different approaches, depending on the problem and the circumstances.

Some important things, however, are common to all science. First, scientists must always be ready to admit mistakes or that their knowledge is incomplete. Scientific ideas are thrown out and replaced if they no longer agree with what is observed. There is no final "truth" in science—only an ongoing quest for better and better explanations of the real world.

Second, all good experiments must be able to be repeated so that other scientists can check the results. It is always possible to make an error, especially in a complicated experiment. So, it is essential that other people, in other places, can perform the same experiment to see if they agree with the findings.

Third, to be effective, science must be shared. In other words, scientists from all over the world must exchange their ideas and results freely through journals and meetings. Not only that, but the general public must be kept informed of what scientists are doing so that they, too, can help to shape the future of scientific research.

To become a better scientist yourself is quite simple. Keep an open mind, ask lots of questions, and most important of all— experiment!

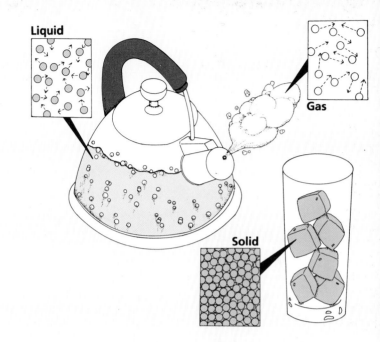

CHAPTER 1

▲ *Molecules exist in solid, liquid, and gas forms.*

Hot Subject

Heat is everywhere: in volcanoes, in icebergs, in your body—in every object in the universe. All matter contains heat.

Like light and sound, heat is a form of energy. This means that it can be used to do work and cause movement. It can also be transferred from one object to another. For example, some of the heat that starts out in the center of the sun eventually reaches the earth and provides us with the warmth we need to live.

Moving Molecules

Almost all the substances around you are made up of molecules. These are very tiny particles that never stop moving.

Whenever you breathe in deeply, you fill

◄ *The heat that comes from a volcano is a form of energy.*

your lungs with about 5 septillion (5 and 24 zeros following it) molecules of oxygen and about 18 septillion molecules of nitrogen. These molecules are racing around at an average speed of about 1,500 feet per second, the speed of a rifle bullet.

As air is heated up, the molecules in it move faster. As it is cooled down, the molecules move slower.

In a gas or a liquid, the molecules are

able to move around freely. In a solid, such as the paper of this page, the molecules are stuck together. However, they can still vibrate back and forth. As a solid is heated up, the vibrations of its molecules get bigger and faster.

In any substance, whether it is a solid, a liquid, or a gas, the speed of its molecules is a measure of how hot or cold it is.

Molecules in Collision

In a liquid or gas, the molecules behave like bumper cars. They keep ramming into one another and bouncing away again. If two different liquids are put together, their molecules immediately start to collide and become mixed up. If one of the liquids is hot, its molecules will smash hard into the molecules of the other liquid and cause them to spread out quickly. On the other hand, if both liquids are cool, their molecules will move more slowly and take longer to mix together.

EXPERIMENT!

Liquid Mix-Up

You Will Need:

- **Two clear glasses**
- **Food coloring**
- **An eyedropper**

What to Do:

Fill one of the glasses with cold water and the other with hot water. Suck up a small amount of food coloring into the eyedropper. Put the end of the eyedropper in the middle of the glass of cold water and gently squeeze out a drop of food coloring. Do the same in the glass of hot water. Compare what happens in the two glasses. Try to explain what you see.

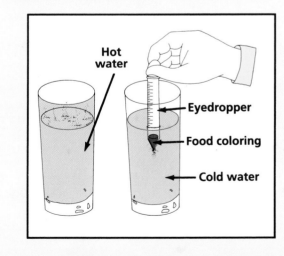

Hot water · Eyedropper · Food coloring · Cold water

*E*X*PERIMENT!*

Hot Air, Cold Air

You Will Need:

- **A balloon**
- **An empty glass bottle**
- **Two large plastic bowls**

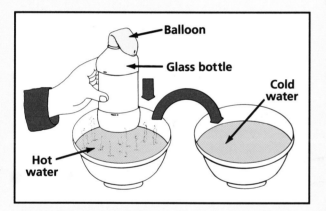

Balloon

Glass bottle

Cold water

Hot water

What to Do:

Take the cap off the bottle and place the balloon over the top. Fill one of the bowls with cold water and the other with hot water. Place the bottle in the hot water. Does anything happen to the balloon? Now place the bottle in the cold water. What happens? Try to explain your observations.

Heat and Gases

As a gas is heated up, its molecules move faster. They collide harder and more often among themselves. They also collide harder and more often with the walls of their container. If the container is made of a stretchy material, such as rubber, it will expand as the gas inside gets hotter. If the container is stiff, as the gas inside heats up, its molecules will not be able to make the container bigger. Instead the gas molecules will just push harder and harder against the walls.

CHAPTER 2

Shrink and Swell

On a hot summer day, telephone wires sag between the poles that hold them up. Yet, on a cold day, the wires are tightly stretched. The reason is that most substances expand as they get hotter, and contract, or shrink, as they cool down.

Metals, when heated, expand more than other kinds of solids do. Because of this, engineers have to be especially careful when designing and building large metal structures. For example, narrow gaps must be left between railroad tracks at regular intervals. This prevents the tracks from buckling during hot weather.

▲ *This outdoor thermometer shows that it is a hot day.*

Lengthening Rods

You Will Need:

- **A sewing needle**
- **A knitting needle**
- **A straw**
- **Three short, fat candles**
- **A baking tray lined with sand**
- **Two wooden blocks**
- **A small, flat mirror**
- **A paper scale, as shown in the diagram**
- **A stopwatch***
- **Several rods of the same size, but made of different metals*** (These could be obtained from a hardware store.)
- **Ice packed into a plastic bag***

Note: Items marked "*" are used only in the "Taking It Further" part of an experiment.

What to Do:

Stick the sewing needle through the straw about a third of the way from one end. Place the mirror on top of one of the wooden blocks. Lay the knitting needle across the two wooden blocks so that one end is touching a wall. Place the needle holding the straw between the mirror and the free end of the knitting needle. Make a paper scale as shown and affix it to a wall or wooden board to show the position of the straw pointer. Arrange the straw so that its long end points straight up at the zero reading. Place the three candles in a line on the baking tray so that they are directly under the knitting needle.

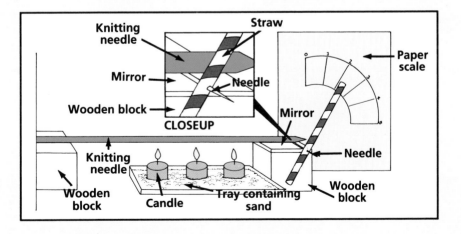

Knitting needle · Straw · Mirror · Needle · Wooden block · **CLOSEUP** · Paper scale · Mirror · Needle · Knitting needle · Wooden block · Candle · Tray containing sand · Wooden block

continued on next page

With the help of an adult, light the candles and start the stopwatch. Note the pointer reading at 1-minute intervals until the reading does not change anymore. Blow out the candles. Plot a graph of pointer readings against time. Can you draw any conclusions from this graph?

Taking It Further:

Repeat the experiment using the rods made of different metals. Make sure the test is fair by heating each rod for the same amount of time. Which metal expands the most? Plot graphs of pointer readings against time for each metal. Do all the graphs look the same?

Allow the metal rods to cool down and return to their original length. At the bottom of the paper scale, mark a new set of readings, as shown, that run in the opposite direction to the top set. Poke a hole in the side of the bag of ice with one of the metal rods. Push the rod all the way through the ice bag and out the other side. Rest the ends of the rod on the wooden blocks as before. Move the straw so that it is pointing at zero on the bottom scale. Start the stopwatch. Note the readings on the bottom scale at 1-minute intervals. What happens to the rod? Draw a graph of your findings. Repeat the experiment using the other rods and compare your results. Does the rod that expanded the most also contract the most?

For more on this, see "Experiment in Depth," page 53, section 1.

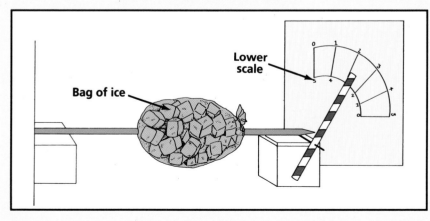

Lower scale

Bag of ice

Warning: Since this experiment involves flames, make sure that an adult is watching. Also be careful not to touch the knitting needle while it is hot. Use pot holders or oven mitts to pick it up about 15 minutes after you have blown out the candles.

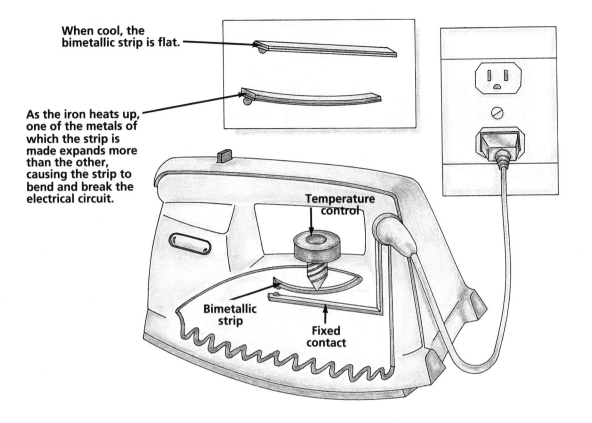

When cool, the bimetallic strip is flat.

As the iron heats up, one of the metals of which the strip is made expands more than the other, causing the strip to bend and break the electrical circuit.

Temperature control

Bimetallic strip

Fixed contact

▲ *How an iron works*

Making Expansion Work

The fact that different metals expand by different amounts can be put to good use. Inside some appliances are two thin strips of different metals joined together to make what is called a "bimetallic strip." When

cold, the bimetallic strip is straight. When heated, however, the metal that expands more bends the strip into a curve. This can be used to make or break an electrical connection. In a clothes iron, for example, a bimetallic strip bends as the iron heats up. Eventually, the strip touches another piece of metal. This completes an electrical circuit that opens a switch so that the iron does not overheat. The position of the strip can be altered by a control to set the temperature of the iron. The same means is used to control central heating systems.

Measuring Hotness
Like solids, liquids and gases also expand when heated and contract when cooled. The amount by which a substance expands or contracts depends on how much its temperature changes. Temperature is the degree of how hot or cold something is, measured with a thermometer.

Most thermometers consist of a narrow, sealed glass tube with a bulb at the end. Inside the bulb is a liquid. In some cases, this is mercury, a silvery liquid metal. The

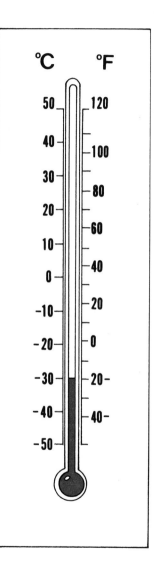

hotter the mercury gets, the more it expands and moves up the tube. Along the tube is a scale. This may show the temperature in degrees Fahrenheit or in degrees Celsius (centigrade). Fahrenheit is used for everyday purposes in the United States. In other parts of the world, though, temperature is normally given in Celsius.

The level the mercury reaches in melting ice is fixed at 0°C or 32°F. In boiling water, a thermometer shows 100°C or 212°F. In between these two fixed points, the scales are laid out in equally spaced divisions.

Thermometers containing alcohol are also common. The alcohol, which is normally clear, is colored red so that it shows up more easily. Alcohol is less expensive than mercury and can be used to measure lower temperatures.

Taking Temperatures

You Will Need:

- **An outdoor thermometer**
- **An indoor thermometer**
- **An oral thermometer**

What to Do:
Set up the outdoor thermometer in a shaded place outside your house or school. Record the temperature every half hour from early morning to late afternoon or evening. Plot a graph of the results. How did the temperature vary during the day? What were the

continued on next page

lowest and the highest temperatures? Repeat this experiment on other days. Do the daily changes in temperature always follow the same pattern?

Use the indoor thermometer to find out the temperature inside your house or classroom. How does the reading change if you put the thermometer near a window, especially when the sun is shining through? Leave the thermometer in the refrigerator for 15 minutes and record the temperature. Do the same in the freezer.

Ask an adult to help you use the oral thermometer. This must be shaken first to make sure that all the mercury is returned to the bulb. Place the thermometer carefully under your tongue and leave it there for 3 minutes. Check the reading. Find out what the temperature of a healthy person should be.

Warning: Always be careful when using thermometers since they are easily broken. If one does break, ask an adult for help in cleaning up the pieces of glass. Never touch mercury or put it in your mouth. It is very poisonous.

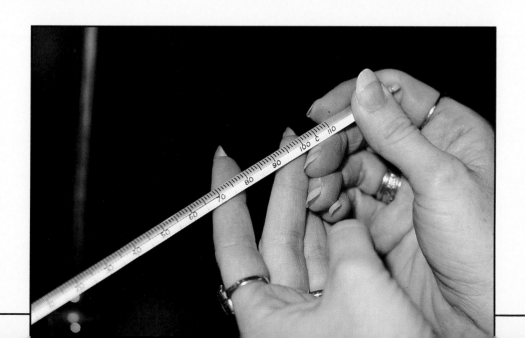

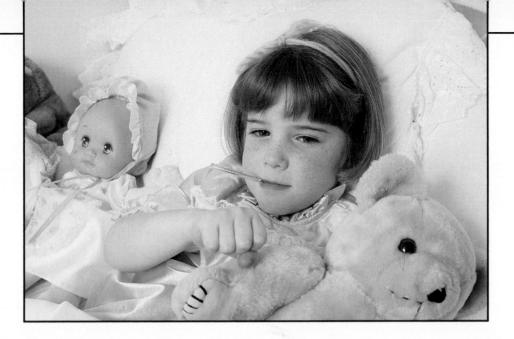

Taking It Further:

With a teacher's help, carry out a survey of the temperatures of people in your class. After each person has had his or her temperature taken, the thermometer must be sterilized. That is, it must be properly cleaned to remove any germs. Your teacher will show you how to do this. Record everyone's temperature to the nearest tenth of a degree. You will probably find that there is some variation in the readings. Count how many people are in each tenth-of-a-degree range from 98° to 99°F (36.3° to 36.9°C). Plot a bar chart to show your results. From this, what would you conclude is a normal temperature range for human beings?

Heat and Temperature

There is an important difference between how hot something is and how much heat it contains. You will already have discovered this if you have bitten into an apple pie from a fast-food restaurant. Although the pastry on the outside and the apple on the inside are at nearly the same temperature, the pastry is easy to eat while the apple can burn your mouth. The reason is that the apple contains much more heat.

Newton's Law

Several hundred years ago, Sir Isaac Newton made an important discovery about how

EXPERIMENT!

The Speed of Cooling

You Will Need:

- **A clear glass pan filled with water**
- **Two thermometers**
- **A stopwatch**

What to Do:

Place one thermometer in the pan and ask an adult to heat the water in the pan to a temperature of about 160°F (70°C). Ask the adult to put the pan on a cool surface. Read the temperature and start the stopwatch. Take the temperature every minute for half an hour. Using the second thermometer, take the temperature of the room. Plot a graph of how much the water cooled each minute (the rate of cooling) against the difference between the water temperature and the temperature of the room. What shape is the graph? What can you deduce from this?

For more on this, see "Experiment in Depth," pages 53-54, section 2.

fast things cool down. He found that the rate of cooling depends on the temperature difference between an object and its surroundings. In other words, the hotter something is, compared with its surroundings, the faster it will cool down. This is known as Newton's Law of Cooling.

Believe It or Not!

THE HIGHEST TEMPERATURES ON RECORD ARE A SIZZLING 134°F (56.1°C) IN DEATH VALLEY, CALIFORNIA, ON JULY 10, 1913, AND 136.4°F (57.4°C) IN THE LIBYAN SAHARA DESERT ON SEPTEMBER 13, 1922.

CHAPTER 3

From Ice Cubes to Saunas

We think of air as being a gas. But if air is cooled down enough, the oxygen and nitrogen in it turn to liquids and eventually to solids. In the same way, we think of iron as being a solid. But if iron is heated to 2,802°F (1,523.5°C) it becomes a liquid, while at 5,252°F (2,871°C) it becomes a gas.

All substances can exist in these three different states: solid, liquid, or gas. The process of going from one form to another is called a change of state.

▲ *Ice cubes: a substance in a solid state*

Shake, Rattle, and Roll

You Will Need:

- **A glass jar**
- **Some dried peas**
- **Red paint and a paintbrush**

What to Do:
Paint about 20 of the peas red and allow the paint to dry. Half fill the jar with peas, including the painted ones. The peas represent the molecules of a substance. The red paint makes it easier for you to follow what happens to one or more individual peas during the course of the experiment. Shake the jar very gently. Keep your eyes on one of the red-painted peas. It will vibrate without changing its position, just like a molecule in a solid does. Now shake the jar slightly harder. Watch what happens. Shake the jar harder still, in different directions. What happens to the pea-molecules?

Dried peas

▲ *Held by human hands, this piece of ice will soon begin to gain heat energy and melt.*

Ice to Steam

Water is one of the commonest and most important chemicals on earth. It is unusual, though, in that it occurs as a solid, a liquid, and a gas in our everyday lives.

The molecules in solid water, or ice, are fixed together in a kind of framework. Al-though they can vibrate, they cannot move around freely. If a block of ice is taken out of a freezer, however, it starts to gain heat energy. This energy makes the ice mol-ecules vibrate faster. Eventually, the mol-ecules gain enough energy to break out of their framework and move around freely. At

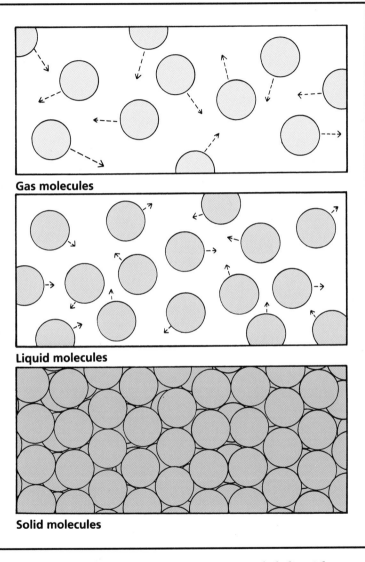

Gas molecules

Liquid molecules

Solid molecules

▲ *Water can appear as a solid, liquid, or gas.*

this point, the ice begins to turn into water. In other words, it melts.

If more heat is given to the water, say by warming it in a pan, the water molecules move even faster. Given enough heat, they will move so quickly that they escape from the surface of the water altogether. The water boils, turning into a gas known as water vapor.

Compare how water turns from a solid to a liquid to a gas with your observations of peas in the "Shake, Rattle, and Roll" experiment.

Changes of State

While a substance is changing state, its temperature remains the same. For example, the temperature of boiling water is 212°F (100°C). Supplying more heat to a pan of boiling water does not raise its temperature; it simply makes the water boil faster.

Melting Ice

You Will Need:

- Some ice cubes
- A plastic bowl
- A thermometer
- A stopwatch

What to Do:

Place the ice cubes in a plastic bowl in a warm room. Put the thermometer carefully in the bowl so that it is sur-rounded by ice. Record the tempera-ture and start the stopwatch. Take further readings of the temperature every 5 minutes. After each reading, gently stir the contents of the bowl. Record the time at which the last of the ice disappears. Continue to record the temperature of the water every 5 minutes until it no longer rises. Plot a graph of time against temperature. Draw a line to show when the last of the ice melted. Can you draw any conclusions from your graph?

In the same way, ice melts at 32°F (0°C). The temperature of a melting ice-water mixture remains the same—32°F (0°C)—until all the ice has melted.

The opposite of melting is freezing. Both happen at the same temperature. For example, freezing water stays at 32°F (0°C) until it has all turned to ice. Only then can it be cooled to lower temperatures.

The opposite of boiling is condensation. This happens when molecules of gas start to stick together and form droplets of liquid. When water in a pan boils, for example, it turns to water vapor, which is an invisible gas. But almost immediately the water vapor condenses into tiny droplets in the air, which we call steam.

Ice crystals will melt quickly into a liquid.▶

Going, Going, Gone

You Will Need:

- **A measuring cup**
- **Containers with different-size openings, such as jars, bowls, and bottles**

What to Do:
Measure out 8 ounces of water and pour it carefully into one of the containers. Repeat this with the other containers. Place all of the containers in the same place in a warm room. Leave them for one week. Pour the contents of each container back into the measuring cup and record the quantity of water for each. What do you notice? Has the amount of water gone down? If so, in which containers has it gone down the most? Try to explain your results.

Repeat the experiment using two containers of the same size and shape. Pour the same amount of water into each. Put one of the containers in a cool place, such as a cupboard. Put the other in a warm place, such as a sunny window ledge. After one week, measure the amount of water remaining. What can you conclude from this?

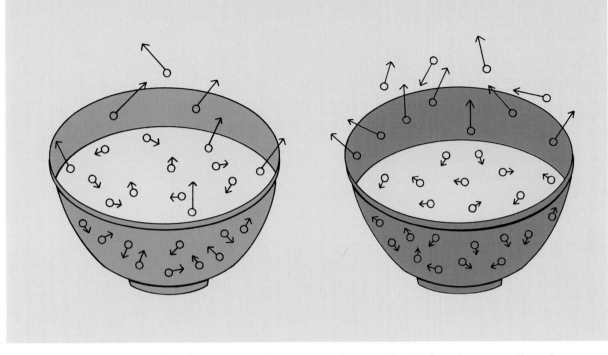

The fastest moving molecules eventually escape from a liquid, leaving only the slower moving molecules behind.

Evaporation

A liquid will turn to gas if it is heated to its boiling point. But a liquid will also slowly turn to gas at lower temperatures. This is called evaporation.

The reason liquids evaporate is that some of the molecules inside them are moving faster than others. The fastest of all have enough energy to escape from the liquid, even though the temperature may be well below the boiling point.

Since a molecule has to break free of a liquid's surface in order to escape, the rate at which a liquid evaporates depends on how much of its surface is exposed to air. Water that is spread out as a shallow puddle, for example, will evaporate much faster than the same amount of water contained in a bottle. The rate of evaporation also increases as the temperature rises.

Cool It!

You Will Need:

- **Two thermometers**
- **A stopwatch**
- **A glass of water**
- **Sticky tape**
- **A thin strip of tissue paper**
- **Cotton thread**
- **An electric fan***

What to Do:

Wrap the top of the strip of tissue paper around the bulb of one of the thermometers. Tie it in place with some thread. Tape the thermometers side by side against a wall or other support. After filling the glass with water, leave it for an hour to come to room temperature. Note the readings on the two thermometers (they should be the same). Dip the free end of the tissue paper into the water, so that the water soaks up to the bulb of the thermometer. Start the stopwatch. Take the readings of both thermometers at 1-minute intervals. Plot a graph of the results. What are your findings? Can you think of an explanation?

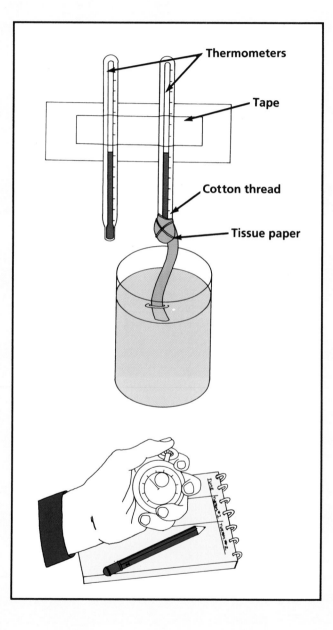

Thermometers

Tape

Cotton thread

Tissue paper

Taking It Further:

Remove the tissue strip from the thermometer. Wait until both thermometers show the same temperature. Attach the tissue strip again and set up the experiment as before. Start the stopwatch. Turn on the fan and point it at the thermometers from a distance of a few feet. Repeat the rest of the experiment as before. Compare your results. Is there any difference? Again, try to explain your observations.

Warning: Never touch an electric appliance, such as the fan in this experiment, if your hands are wet. You may receive a dangerous shock.

Cooling by Evaporation

The temperature of a substance depends on the average energy of all its molecules. If the fastest molecules get away, then the average energy of the molecules that are left will be lower—and the substance will be cooler. For this reason, evaporation causes a liquid to cool down.

When we are hot, we sweat. As the fastest water molecules in the sweat escape, they lower the temperature of the remaining liquid. This, in turn, helps to cool our skin and the blood that flows beneath it.

If the air over an evaporating liquid is still, a tiny cloud of water vapor collects near the liquid's surface. This makes it harder for other molecules to escape. However, if the air is moving, the cloud of water vapor is blown away. This enables other molecules in the liquid to escape more easily so that the rate of evaporation—and the rate of cooling—are increased. To see this idea at work, lick the

back of your hand; then blow across it. Blow gently at first and then harder. What do you feel?

Inside Freezers

Cooling by evaporation gives us a way to make ice and to preserve food by freezing it. Look behind a refrigerator and you will see some twisting pipes behind a line of metal "fins." The pipes contain a substance called Freon, which changes very easily from liquid to vapor and back again.

The Freon starts its journey around the refrigerator by being squeezed out of a pump [1] as a vapor at high pressure. It passes up through the pipes at the back of the refrigerator [2], losing heat as it turns into a liquid. The metal fins are designed to get rid of this heat, which is why they feel warm. Next, the Freon is squirted through a

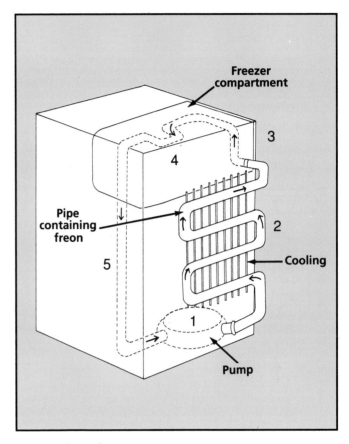

▲ *Inside a freezer*

◀*When we exercise, we get hot. And when we get hot, we sweat.*

narrow opening [3] into a wider pipe that passes around the inside of the freezer compartment [4] and the rest of the refrigerator [5]. This causes the Freon to evaporate and cool its surroundings. Finally, the Freon returns to the pump to begin its journey all over again.

Believe It or Not!

REMAINING FULLY CLOTHED WHILE IN THE DESERT MAY BE UNCOMFORTABLE, BUT BY SLOWING THE EVAPORATION OF BODY WATER, IT CAN SAVE YOUR LIFE.

CHAPTER 4

Passing the Heat Along

Leave a metal spoon in a cup of coffee and quite soon the handle of the spoon will become hot. This is an example of heat traveling by conduction.

We can understand why the end of the spoon gets hot by once again thinking about molecules. The fast-moving molecules of water in the coffee bump into the part of the spoon that is next to the hot liquid. This makes the metal molecules of the spoon vibrate harder so that the metal heats up. Quickly the vibrations are passed on, from molecule to molecule, up the handle of the spoon.

Why does this spoon become hot? ▶

A Test of Conductors

You Will Need:

- **Copper and steel wire of the same thickness**
- **Wire made from other metals of the same thickness***
- **A stopwatch**
- **Three short, fat candles**
- **Vaseline or melted candle wax**
- **Paper clips**
- **Two thumbtacks**
- **A ruler**
- **Two wooden blocks**

What to Do:

Twist the ends of the two wires together, making sure that the twisted part of each wire is the same length. Support the wires between the two wooden blocks and fasten their free ends to one of the blocks with thumb-tacks. Attach paper clips one inch apart along each wire, using Vaseline or drops of melted wax from a candle. Ask an adult to help you with this. Space the three candles evenly under the middle of the twisted wires and light them. Observe what happens. Time how long it takes for each paper clip along each wire to fall off. Plot a graph of time versus distance. From your results, decide which metal is the better conductor.

Taking It Further:

Continue the experiment with wire made from other metals. Are the best conductors also those metals that expanded most in the experiment "Lengthening Rods" on page 13?

For more on this, see "Experiment in Depth," page 54, section 3.

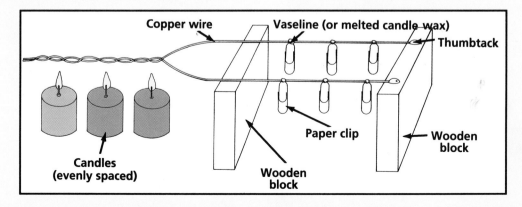

Copper wire — Vaseline (or melted candle wax) — Thumbtack — Paper clip — Wooden block — Candles (evenly spaced) — Wooden block

Conductors and Insulators

Substances through which heat can travel
easily are said to be good conductors.
Metals are the best conductors. That is why
we use them for making such things as
saucepans and radiators. It also explains
why metals usually feel cool to the touch. If
a metal object is at a lower temperature
than your body, it will quickly carry heat
away from your skin when you touch it. The
opposite is true if the metal is warmer than
you are. Then the metal will quickly give up
its heat to your skin so that it feels hot to
the touch.

A substance through which heat cannot
travel well is called an insulator. Air, for
example, is a very good insulator.

▲ *Metals are good conductors.*

38

Can the Heat Get Through?

You Will Need:

- A rubber hot-water bottle
- Pieces of wood, plastic, paper, cardboard, cork, and woolen and cotton materials. Stack each of these so that they are all of roughly the same thickness.

What to Do:

Fill the hot-water bottle with hot (but not boiling) water and lay it on a table. Place the piece of wood on the bottle and leave it there for 5 minutes. Put your hand on top of the wood. Record whether it feels "very warm," "quite warm," "warm," or "cool." Repeat this with the plastic, paper, and other substances. From your results, make a list of the materials, with the best conductors at the top and the best insulators at the bottom. You may occasionally need to replace the hot water so that the hot-water bottle is at more or less the same temperature throughout the experiment.

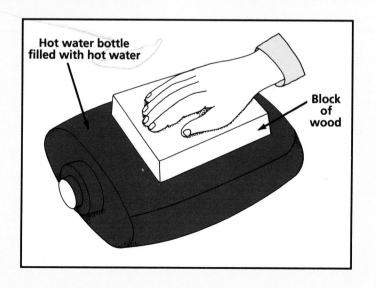

Hot water bottle filled with hot water

Block of wood

Protecting the Space Shuttle

As the orbiter of the space shuttle returns to earth, it plunges through the upper atmosphere at very high speed. Without proper protection this would cause the metal hull of the craft to melt. Scientists have therefore developed a special insulating material, containing silicon, which can be made into thin, lightweight tiles. These tiles are used to cover the orbiter's underside, nose, and wing tips.

A space-shuttle tile is such a good insulator that one side can be held in bare hands while the opposite side is red-hot. It can withstand temperatures of up to 2,300°F (1,260°C).

Pockets of Air

Air is one of the best of all insulators. This means that a good insulator can be made by trapping little pockets of air within a substance. The insulation that is often

▲ *Our homes are surrounded with materials.*

found around hot-water tanks or in the attics of houses works in this way. It holds still air between the fibers of a fluffy material.

You can use this idea to help stay warm in winter. By dressing in many layers of thinner clothing instead of wearing one or

Thermal Wrappings

You Will Need:

- A jar with a metal lid
- Two thermometers
- Play-Doh
- Various materials with which to wrap the jar, such as aluminum foil, cloth, cotton, and newspaper
- A plastic jug
- A stopwatch

What to Do:

Ask an adult to make a hole in the middle of the metal lid of the jar, just big enough for one of the thermometers to fit through. Push the thermometer through the hole and seal any gap with some Play-Doh. Wrap the sides and base of the jar with aluminum foil, leaving enough foil free at the top to cover the lid. Fill the jug with hot water from a hot-water faucet (or ask an adult to heat up some water for you). Measure the temperature of this water with the second thermometer. Immediately fill the jar with hot water from the jug. Put on the lid, cover the lid with foil, and start the stopwatch. After 10 minutes, take off the foil wrapping and record the thermometer reading. Throw out the water and wrap the jar with a different material. Fill the jug again with fresh hot water and make sure that this is at the same temperature as before. Repeat the experiment as with the foil. Do the same with the other wrapping materials that you have. Which provided the best insulation?

Taking It Further:

Try different combinations of wrappings to see if these insulate the jar better. For example, you could put some cotton between two layers of newspaper.

For more on this, see "Experiment in Depth," pages 54-55, section 4.

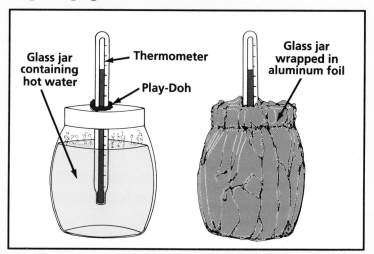

Glass jar containing hot water — Thermometer — Play-Doh — Glass jar wrapped in aluminum foil

two thick items, you trap more air between the layers and so prevent your body heat from escaping. Boots and coats designed for use in low temperatures are themselves made from many layers for this purpose.

▲ *Well-insulated clothing keeps us warm in the coldest weather.*

Believe It or Not!

DURING AN EXPEDITION TO THE NORTH POLE IN 1986, EXPLORER ANN BANCROFT FELL THROUGH A HOLE IN THE ICE. AFTER HAVING CHANGED HER WET CLOTHES AT -22°F (-30°C), SHE TOOK TWO DAYS TO WARM UP.

CHAPTER 5

Convection's Ups and Downs

If you hold your hand over a hot radiator, you can feel warmth on your skin. In the previous chapter, though, we said that air is a poor conductor. So, how can heat from the radiator travel through the air to warm your hand? The answer is that the heat does not travel by conduction, but by a different process called convection.

The air molecules that collide with a radiator pick up heat energy from the hot metal. This makes the air molecules move faster and farther apart. Since the warm air around the radiator is now lighter, it rises. Cooler air from other parts of the room moves in to take its place. As the warm air rises, it loses heat energy, becomes heavier, and falls again. Eventually, it returns to the radiator to be heated once more.

▲ *In order for hot-air balloons to stay aloft, the air needs to remain hot.*

Rising Rice

You Will Need:

- **Some grains of uncooked rice**
- **A clear glass pan**
- **A crystal of potassium permanganate***
- **A glass beaker* (the kind used in a school laboratory)**
- **Tweezers***
- **A Bunsen burner* (used to supply heat to experiments in a laboratory)**

What to Do:

Only attempt this experiment with adult help. Ask the adult to partly fill the pan with cold water and to place it on a stove to heat. As the water begins to warm up, ask the adult to sprinkle some grains of rice in the water at the edge of the pan. From a safe distance of several feet, watch what happens. How does the rice move? Try to explain what you see. What happens to the rice as the pan is allowed to cool?

Taking It Further:

In a school laboratory, this experiment can be done in a different way by using a crystal of the purple chemical, potassium permanganate. Partly fill a beaker with cold water. With tweezers, carefully place a crystal of potassium permanganate at the bottom of the beaker near to one side. The teacher will then put the beaker on a stand and light a Bunsen burner while you stand at a safe distance. Watch what happens as the teacher heats the beaker just below the crystal. Try to explain what you observe.

Warning: You must have adult help with these experiments. Potassium permanganate is poisonous if swallowed. It will stain clothing when dissolved.

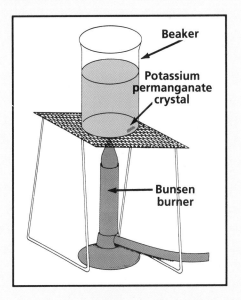

Beaker

Potassium permanganate crystal

Bunsen burner

Convection Currents

Convection can happen in both liquids and gases, but not in solids. Can you think why?

In conduction, heat flows directly from a hot object to a cold one. In convection, however, heat is moved around by a current of liquid or gas.

The Weather Machine

On a warm day the sun heats up the land, which in turn heats the air above it. The warm air rises, allowing cooler, heavier air to move in and take its place.

On a large scale, this process gives rise to winds around the world. Warm tropical air rises to a height of several miles and moves off in the direction of the poles. Cold air over the poles sinks and moves toward the tropics. In between, there are regions of rising and sinking air. These circulating patterns occur all the time. The wind and weather at any place on earth, however,

EXPERIMENT!

How a Room Warms Up

You Will Need:

- **A small- or medium-size room containing a radiator**
- **Several thermometers**
- **A stopwatch**

What to Do:

The room should be cool to begin with—60°F (16°C). Place the thermometers in various parts of the room: high up, low down, near the radiator, and far away from it. Draw a plan of the room, showing the locations of the thermometers. Record their temperatures. Turn on the radiator and start the stopwatch. Every 10 minutes record the temperatures shown on all the thermometers. Do this for a period of about 2 hours. Draw graphs to show how the readings on each thermometer changed with time. Which parts of the room heated up fastest? Was the temperature of the room fairly even at the end of the experiment? Are the results as you expected?

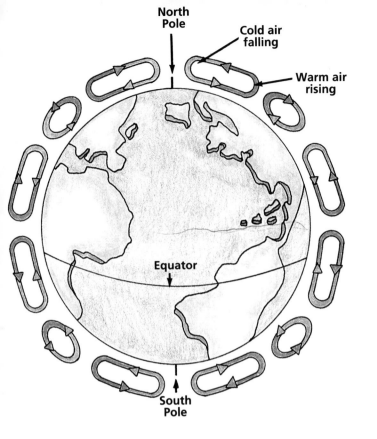

North Pole

Cold air falling

Warm air rising

Equator

South Pole

Believe It or Not!

WELCOME TO ICELAND HOME OF GLACIERS, ICE, AND BANANAS!

HUGE GREENHOUSES IN ICELAND ARE KEPT WARM USING HOT WATER THAT IS PUMPED FROM UNDER THE EARTH. THIS ALLOWS ICELAND TO BE ONE OF EUROPE'S BIGGEST PRODUCERS OF BANANAS.

may vary a great deal from day to day. This is because the circulation of air is affected by many different factors, including the earth's spin, obstructions such as mountains, and seasonal changes in the sun's heating.

CHAPTER 6

Rays of Warmth

Stand outside on a warm summer day and you can feel the sun's heat on your face. But how does it reach you? There is nothing but 93 million miles of empty space between the sun and the earth. Heat can only travel by conduction or convection where there is matter. To cross empty space, it must move by a different means. The third method by which heat moves is called radiation.

Heat radiation, like light, consists of waves. Heat waves are also known as infrared waves. The only difference between infrared and ordinary light is that the waves of infrared are farther apart. Both infrared and light waves travel at about

▲ *The sun is 93 million miles away from the earth.*

186,000 miles per second in empty space. At this speed, they take just over 8 minutes to go from the sun to the earth.

Warmth in
Three Ways

You Will Need:

● A hot-water bottle

What to Do:
Ask an adult to fill the hot-water bottle with hot (but not boiling) water and to hold the bottle level. Touch the bottle. Next place your hand about an inch above the bottle. Finally hold your hand about an inch below the bottle. Try to decide how the heat reaches your skin in each case. Remember that heat can travel by more than one way at once. Explain why, when you hold your hand below the bottle, the heat that you feel cannot have traveled either by conduction or convection.

Heat Rays and Matter
The amount of heat radiation soaked up by a substance depends on what type of substance it is. Dark, rough materials are good absorbers of infrared. Light, smooth materials, however, bounce back, or reflect, most of the heat radiation that falls on them. For example, a dull, black surface will feel much hotter on a sunny day than a shiny, white surface.

A material that reflects light like a mirror, such as metal foil, will also reflect most of the heat waves that strike it. This explains why spacecraft, which must remain cool inside even in permanent sunlight, are often wrapped in shiny metal foil.

Soaking Up the Heat

You Will Need:

- Four thermometers
- A sheet of black paper
- A sheet of white paper
- A sheet of clear cellophane
- A sheet of aluminum foil
- Other colored paper and materials*

What to Do:

Lay the four thermometers near one another on a flat surface in the sunshine. Record their temperatures. Cover each thermometer with one of the sheets and leave them for about 20 minutes. Remove each sheet in turn and quickly read the temperature of the thermometer. Under which sheet was it the hottest and under which the coolest? What does this tell you about how well the different sheets absorb heat radiation?

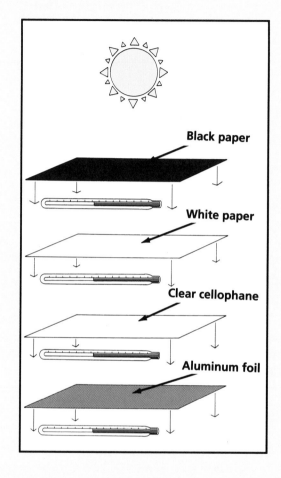

Black paper

White paper

Clear cellophane

Aluminum foil

Taking It Further:

Experiment with sheets of other materials and colors. For example, does green paper absorb more heat radiation than yellow? Compare rough paper with smooth paper of the same color. Based on your results, what color clothes do you think it would be best to wear on a hot, sunny day?

Experiment!

Under Glass

You Will Need:

- A glass jar
- A clear plastic container
- Two thermometers

What to Do:

Lay the two thermometers next to each other outside in the sunshine. Take their readings. Place the jar over one of the thermometers. Read both thermometers every 15 minutes for two hours. Plot a graph of your results. Repeat the experiment with the clear plastic container instead of the jar. What can you deduce from your findings?

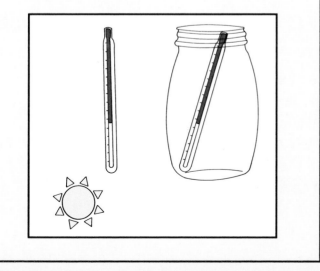

A Trap for Sunlight

Glass will let both light waves and heat waves from the sun pass easily through it. Any object that is under glass will absorb some of the sun's heat. This object will then give off heat waves of its own. But the new heat waves will be farther apart than those that came directly from the sun. These longer heat waves cannot pass through the glass, so they are trapped inside. As a result, the temperature of the air and objects under the glass rises.

This is how greenhouses work. They trap heat from the sun and use it to speed the growth of plants. You can make a miniature greenhouse simply by putting a jar over a patch of grass on a lawn. A few days later the grass under the jar will have grown taller than the surrounding grass, because it has been kept warmer.

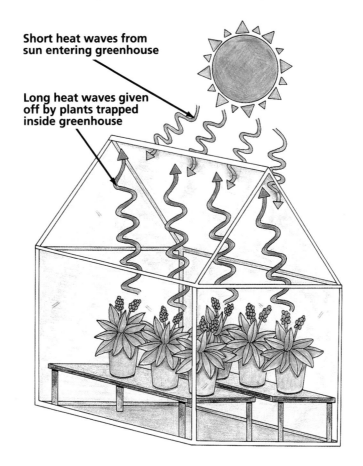

Short heat waves from sun entering greenhouse

Long heat waves given off by plants trapped inside greenhouse

▲ *How a greenhouse works*

The Earth: A Giant Greenhouse

Some gases work like the glass in a greenhouse. In other words, they let heat radiation from the sun reach the earth, but block the longer heat waves traveling back up from the land and sea. One of these greenhouse gases is carbon dioxide. This is a substance that we breathe out and that plants take in. Plants turn the carbon dioxide into oxygen, which we need in order to live.

One of the problems at present is that

many human activities produce large amounts of carbon dioxide. These activities include burning gas in car engines and burning coal and oil in electricity-making power stations. At the same time, people are cutting down large areas of forest in places such as Brazil, so there are fewer plants to remove carbon dioxide from the atmosphere. The result is that the amount of carbon dioxide in the atmosphere is steadily going up. This is increasing the greenhouse effect and may soon cause average temperatures around the world to rise. Many scientists say that this is already happening and that we must take immediate steps to cut the amount of carbon dioxide and other greenhouse gases going into the air.

This section looks at some of the experiments described in this book in more detail.

1. Lengthening Rods, pages 13-14. Although metals expand more than other solids, the amount by which they expand is still very small. For example, iron expands by 0.0001 (one ten-thousandth) of its length for every degree Celsius rise in its temperature. This means that an iron rail 45 feet long would become just over 1-1/2 inches longer if its temperature rose by 86°F (30°C). The gaps between rails on a railroad track are to allow for this.

In our experiment, the increases in length of the rods are much less than an inch. For example, if an iron or steel rod starts out 12 inches (30.4 cm) long and has its temperature raised by 212°F (100°C), it will only lengthen by 0.12 inches (0.3 cm).

This is such a small amount that it would be difficult to observe if a pointer were simply fixed to the end of the rod. By using the needle, mirror, straw, and curved scale as described, however, the amount by which the rod grows is magnified. This also makes it easier to observe differences in the expansion of different metals. Such methods of making small effects more noticeable are often used in experiments and in measuring equipment.

2. The Speed of Cooling, page 20. This experiment can be extended to other substances. For example, what happens to the shape of the cooling curve if you use hot coffee, syrup, or hot cereal?

In the section "Heat and Temperature," the point is made that some things contain more heat than others, even though they are at the same temperature. By comparing the way different liquids, such as water and hot cereal, cool, can you say which contain the most heat? Try to explain the reason for this. Follow up your experiments by looking for information in other books and holding a classroom discussion.

3. A Test of Conductors, page 36.

You may also wish to try comparing two wires of the same metal but of different thickness. Does heat travel faster along a thinner wire of copper than a thicker one? If so, how much faster? For instance, if one wire is half as thick as another, does heat travel twice as fast along it?

Try making up your own questions and then devising an experiment to answer them. You may find, as scientists often do, that while one experiment may help solve a particular problem, it leads to other interesting problems and further ideas for experiments.

4. Thermal Wrappings, page 40.

In designing an experiment it is always important to make it as fair as possible. In other words, apart from those things you want to study, all other conditions should remain unchanged. For example, in this experiment, the thicknesses of the wrapping materials used should be the same. Otherwise it would be impossible to say whether one wrapper kept in more heat than another because it was made of better insulating material or simply because it was thicker.

For the experiment to be fair, you must also make sure that all the wrappings completely cover the jar. Even a small opening will allow heat to escape without first having to pass through the material surrounding the glass. This kind of care is important in all experiments, since without it you bring in other factors that can have an unknown effect upon your results.

Try to think of ways to improve this experiment or extend it. For instance, in a class project, you might try to design an experiment to test the insulating properties of materials used in building.

GLOSSARY

alcohol—a clear liquid, with a low freezing point, that is commonly used in both indoor and outdoor thermometers. It is often stained red to make it easily visible.

bimetallic strip—two different metals joined together to form a long, thin strip. When heated, one of the metals expands more than the other and so causes the strip to bend. This can be used as a means to control the heating and cooling of various devices.

Celsius—one of the two main scales of temperature in common use. On the Celsius scale, the freezing point of water is 0° and the boiling point of water is 100°.

change of state—This happens when a substance goes from one of its three possible states—solid, liquid, or gas—to another.

condensation—the process of changing from a gas to a liquid.

conduction—one of the three ways by which heat can travel from one place to another. It involves the transfer of heat energy from one molecule to the next molecule.

conductor—a substance or object that lets heat pass easily through it.

convection—one of the three ways by which heat can travel from one place to another. It involves the movement of parts of a gas or liquid as they become heated up and cooled down again.

energy—the ability to do work or cause movement.

evaporation—the process of changing from a liquid to a gas at temperatures below the boiling point of the liquid.

Fahrenheit—one of the two main scales of temperature in common use. On the Fahrenheit scale, the freezing point of water is 32° and the boiling point of water is 212°.

Freon—a substance used in refrigerators that changes easily from liquid to gas and back again.

infrared—heat radiation.

insulator—a substance or object that does not let heat pass easily through it.

mercury—the only metal that is a liquid at normal room temperature. Used commonly in thermometers, it has the advantage that it will not stick to glass.

molecule—the smallest part of a substance that can exist and still have the properties of that substance.

oral thermometer—a kind of mercury thermometer used to take the temperature of the human body. Its scale covers only the range of temperatures found in human beings.

radiation—one of the three ways by which heat can travel from one place to another. It involves the movement of heat by electromagnetic waves.

steam—tiny droplets of water that form when water vapor condenses.

thermometer—a device used for measuring temperature.

water vapor—the gas that water turns into. Compare this with steam.

INDEX

59

About the Author

Dr. David Darling is the author of many science books for young readers, including the Dillon Press Discovering Our Universe, World of Computers, and Could You Ever? series. Dr. Darling, who holds degrees in physics and astronomy, has also written many articles for *Astronomy* and *Odyssey* magazines. His first science book for adult readers, *Deep Time* (1989), has been described by Arthur C. Clarke as "brilliant." He currently lives with his family in England, where he writes and lectures to students in schools.